ROCKY MOUNTAIN

NATIONAL PARK

A VISUAL
INTERPRETATION

includes
"The Rooftop of America"
by
George Wuerthner

SIERRA PRESS, INC.

ROCKY MOUNTAIN
NATIONAL PARK

A VISUAL
INTERPRETATION

includes
"The Rooftop of America"
by
George Wuerthner

Ferns and aspens, autumn near Bear Lake.

Elk (wapiti) in Horseshoe Park, winter.

Forest, summer in Paradise Park.

FRONT COVER: Alpine tundra and Longs Peak from Trail Ridge.
BACK COVER: Longs Peak and fog seen from Moraine Park.

ISBN O-939365-43-X

Printed in Singapore.
First Edition 1995.

ACKNOWLEDGEMENTS

We would like to take this opportunity to thank the many photographers who made their imagery available to us during the editing of this title. While no single image can effectively replace the actual experience of being there, we believe the visual story told by the images contained in this volume do tell the story of seasonal change and process more effectively than what the visitor would experience while on vacation. On behalf of those who will see this book, we thank you for sharing the fruits of your labors.
We would also like to thank Heidi Knudson of the Rocky Mountain Nature Association and Jeff Maugans of Rocky Mountain National Park, as well as their staffs, for their invaluable assistance in the creation of this book—Thank You!

DEDICATION

This book is a visual tribute to the insight of those few who saw the wisdom of setting aside such a tract of land for the future, without regard for personal gain. That Rocky Mountain National Park and the National Park Service have become models for more than 130 countries from around the world is all the proof that is necessary to confirm their wisdom. We can only hope our own use is consistent with this wisdom and in no way contributes to the degradation of this most extraordinary legacy.
In this spirit, let us all pledge to continue to work, and sacrifice, for the greater good of places such as Rocky Mountain National Park.

SIERRA PRESS, INC.

4988 Gold Leaf Drive, Mariposa, CA 95338

CONTENTS

Trail Ridge Road and Longs Peak.

The Rooftop of America
by
George Wuerthner

From out on the eastern plains of Colorado, I can pick out the snowy summit of Longs Peak, more than one hundred miles away. I've fantasized about the cool, green land the peak heralds many times while driving across the seemingly endless, hot, parched, and bronzed plains of eastern Colorado. The highest summit within today's Rocky Mountain National Park, Longs Peak is named for Major Stephen Long, who in 1820 mapped what was then the unknown western reaches of United States territory. Like me, Long was tantalized by the promise of its chill heights, as he trudged across the dusty plains, which he characterized as the "Great American Desert." Though he never did get very close to the mountain that now bears his name, Long was the first white explorer to draw attention to these mountains, which today are visited by three million people annually.

Climbers on "The Diamond", east face of Longs Peak.

EARLY HISTORY

Centuries before the area around Longs Peak was given park status, it was the province of Native Americans. Paleo-Indians hunted bison in the highlands after the retreat of ice age glaciers more than 10,000 years ago. By the 1700s and early 1800s, Ute and Arapaho Indians were traversing the ridges in what is today's park, en route to hunting grounds on the plains and in large, open mountain valleys, such as Middle and North parks, where they stalked bison, elk, and deer. Indeed, at least five major Indian trails cross Rocky Mountain National Park, with Trail Ridge, now a paved highway, among the best known.

After Long's passage, a few other itinerant trappers and frontiersmen passed through the region, but it was Joel Estes who laid claim to being the area's first permanent white settler. He homesteaded his namesake valley, Estes Park, in 1860 and spent seven years trying to run cattle in the high country. However, when he realized the high, open valley (or park) might produce more dollars as a vacation destination than as a cattle ranch, he converted one of his cabins into a guest facility and launched the first tourist venture in what would become Rocky Mountain National Park.

Estes didn't have to wait long before the area became fashionable with those interested in outdoor pursuits. In 1868, Civil War hero Major John Wesley Powell, who shortly after led the first successful journey on the Colorado River through the Grand Canyon, was a member of the first party to scale Longs Peak. In 1872, Lord Dunraven became so entranced with the valley of Estes Park that through purchase, as well as fraudulent means, he obtained control of nearly 15,000 acres. He maintained the land as a private hunting preserve for himself. Dunraven further popularized the future park after he commissioned the famous artist Albert Bierstadt (for whom Bierstadt Lake is named) to paint majestic landscapes of the area. By 1874, a regular stage run between Longmount and Estes Park was in operation, bringing even greater numbers of sightseers and adventurers.

THE PARK IDEA TAKES SHAPE

Enos Mills, a self-taught naturalist and innkeeper who settled

---

near Estes Park in 1884, is credited with proposing national park status for the area. By 1909, he had made a proposal to establish the entire Front Range, from Pikes Peak to the Wyoming border, as a national park. He was even commissioned by Theodore Roosevelt to travel the country to lecture on the idea. Unfortunately, Mills was too far ahead of his time, and mining, ranching, and logging interests successfully scuttled the original park proposal. He came back with a greatly scaled-down version that sought to protect only the highest and grandest peaks in the Front Range. In 1915, President Woodrow Wilson followed Mills's proposal and signed a bill establishing Rocky Mountain National Park. In 1975, the United Nations declared the park an International Biosphere Reserve, in recognition of its international biological significance.

Today the park encompasses more than 265,000 acres of the Front Range, plus portions of two spur ranges—the Mummy Range and the Never Summer Range. True to its name, the park includes some very high-elevation real estate. Within this relatively small knot of mountains are some one hundred and twelve named peaks exceeding 10,000 feet.

Seventy-six summits break the 12,000-foot barrier and sixteen peaks, including Longs Peak (14,255 feet), exceed 13,000 feet. It's no wonder that some call Rocky Mountain National Park "the rooftop of America."

Although more than 10,000 people a year attempt to scale Longs Peak, the majority of visitors settle for a less rigorous ascent of these mountains by driving Trail Ridge Road, the highest continuously paved road in America. For more than eleven miles the highway travels above timberline, and at its highest point the road reaches 12,183 feet. On Trail Ridge, you view many of the park's mountains from above!

THE GEOLOGICAL SETTING

Trail Ridge Road is one of the easiest ways to get a look at the geological lay of the land. Looking off into Forest Canyon, for example, one sees the nearly linear fault, or break in the earth's crust, that separates Trail Ridge from the mountains beyond. Closer at hand are the rocks surrounding the Forest Canyon overlook. These grainy, hard outcrops are granite, a form of igneous rock created deep within the earth and composed of cooled magma, or molten rock. These granites are more than 1.3

Aspen leaves and pine needles carpet the forest floor.

billion years old. Other rocks seen along Trail Ridge and on the other high peaks of the park include 1.7-billion-year-old schists and gneisses—both metamorphized sedimentary rocks.

The rocks atop the high peaks of the park once sat at the base of mountains that erosion removed long ago. The overlying younger rocks were stripped away, leaving behind a relatively level plain, the remnants of which can be seen in the gently undulating terrain on Trail Ridge and on the five-acre summit of Longs Peak. Ironically, such level surfaces characterize many of Rocky Mountain's "peaks," with one peak appropriately named Flattop Mountain.

The process of turning mountain roots into mountain tops began with the uplift of the entire Rocky Mountain chain about 50 million years ago. This initial rise was followed, some 25 to 30 million years ago, by volcanic eruptions originating in today's Never Summer Range. Great volumes of ash and other materials were spewed forth, with hot ash flowing across what is now the Kawuneeche Valley, before coming to rest near Lava Cliffs on Trail Ridge Road. Here, the ash cooled and welded into volcanic tuff, which makes up the

rock exposed in the cliffs.

Mineralization associated with these periods of volcanic activity spurred some early mining activity in the 1870s in the North Fork of the Colorado River valley, but prospectors met with little success. Since the granites, schists, and gneisses that make up the majority of what is now Rocky Mountain National Park lacked gold or other valuable metals, the region remained undeveloped until it was set aside for preservation after the turn of the century. All that remains of this earlier era are the abandoned miner's cabins at sites such as Lulu City.

THE ICE COMETH

Geological events control the kinds of rocks found in the park, but they don't explain the rugged canyons, lakes, and valleys that give Rocky Mountain its trademark look. The finishing touches to the mountain scenery were added less than 2 million years ago, when ice age glaciers sculpted and scraped the ancient rocks into approximately their present form.

About 15,000 years ago, most of the higher parts of the park

Bighorn sheep (ewe).

were cloaked in ice, although the tops of the highest summits, such as Longs Peak, stuck out above the ice as unglaciated peaks known as nunataks. An ice cap centered on the Continental Divide produced numerous valley glaciers, which poured down the existing stream valleys. The ice carved these canyons into broad U-shaped valleys, such as Wild Basin, Glacier Gorge, Forest Canyon, the upper Cache la Poudre, and the Upper North Fork of the Colorado River.

Most of these glacially carved valleys were previously carved by running water into a V-shape, then enlarged and sculpted by ice into U-shaped valleys. Both glacial- and water-carved valleys follow ancient faults in the bedrock. This is one reason for their often straight courses. For example, both Forest Canyon and the Kawuneeche Valley are fault-defined, linear valleys later widened and smoothed by the passage of glacial ice.

Some of the glaciers originating in what is now the park were immense. The Kawuneeche Valley once held a twenty-mile-long glacier, which flowed from the Cache la Poudre headwaters all the way to Shadow Mountain Lake. A similarly large,

thirteen-mile-long, 2,500-foot thick, tongue of ice poured down the upper Big Thompson River valley through Forest Canyon. These large glaciers disappeared at the end of the last major ice age, but a cooling period roughly 400 years ago activated another minor growth of glacial ice, which formed among some of the highest basins. Since that time, most of these tiny ice bodies have melted, although there are still five relict, miniature glaciers that remain.

Other glacial features abound in the park. Moraine Valley and Horseshoe Valley were former glacial lakes, dammed by moraines (the dirt and boulders piled by advancing and retreating glaciers). The lakes eventually filled to become wet meadows. Most of the other one hundred and fifty-plus lakes in the park occupy glacial cirques. Grand Lake, just outside the park and the largest natural lake in Colorado, was formed when waters were backed up behind a moraine. A good place to view a glacial moraine is Aspenglen Campground, which rests on a moraine that once backed up a lake in Horseshoe Park.

Glaciers not only shaped the major features of the park but also

Bighorn sheep (ram).

left a legacy affecting the distribution of plants and animals. For example, well-drained moraines are often dominated by drought-resistant trees such as ponderosa pine, while the fine soils left behind after glacial lakes have drained tend to be dominated by wetland species such as sedges and willows. Examples of this can be seen in Wild Basin and Moraine Park.

CLIMATIC INFLUENCES

Although a few relict glaciers still reside in some of the higher cirque basins, the overall precipitation affecting the park today would never support the formation of new glaciers. It's just too dry. Storms, which come predominantly from the west, dump most of their moisture long before reaching Rocky Mountain's high, eastside peaks. An average of sixteen inches of precipitation falls on the eastern portion of the park, while twenty inches is recorded for the slightly moister western slope. Even the highest ridges tend to get less than twenty-five inches annually. First-time winter visitors are frequently surprised by the lack of snow. Often the valley at Estes Park will be entirely free of snow most of the winter, even though the city lies above 7,500 feet in elevation.

Most winter snowfall results from Pacific storm fronts, with accompanying temperatures that are relatively mild. However, a couple of times every winter, frigid air masses from the Arctic will invade from the northern Great Plains, dropping temperatures below zero and bringing the pipe-bursting, numbing temperatures that people often associate with the Rockies.

Summer days are typically sunny in the morning with thunderstorms forming in the afternoon. The storms result from moist "monsoon" air masses that regularly sweep in from the Gulf of Mexico. These air masses are driven upward into giant cumulus clouds—thunderheads that seem to grow almost magically from the highest peaks. Autumn brings some of the best weather, with crisp nights and clear, warm, sunny days. For this reason, autumn is also the best time for climbing the higher peaks in the park because afternoon thunderstorms, and the lightning that accompanies them, are unusual. Indeed, September is the sunniest month of the year.

But if Rocky Mountain has a climatic trademark, it is wind. Several buildings in the park, including the Alpine Visitor

Center, are anchored by large, heavy logs piled on the roofs. Hurricane-force gales blowing more than two hundred miles per hour have been recorded on the summit of Longs Peak, and winds of one hundred miles per hour or more are common in the valleys. You can see the effects of the wind in the "krummholtz"—twisted, contorted trees with branches all on the leeward side—that cling to the rocks near timberline.

Many of these winds are known locally as "chinooks." They tend to be very dry and warm. They were called "snow eaters" by the Indians because of their ability to "sublimate" snow, meaning that water would change directly from its solid to its vaporous form without going through the intermediary phase of being liquid. When a chinook starts blowing, the wind speed may increase to fifty to sixty miles per hour, while air temperature often rises forty to fifty degrees in a matter of hours.

MAJOR PLANT COMMUNITIES

Soil, wind, moisture, slope aspect, and elevation all influence plant communities. From 7,000 to 9,000 feet, on the driest, sunniest slopes, are grasslands intermixed with open, savannalike forests of ponderosa

pine. With red, scaly bark, bracts of three longish needles, and rather large cones, the ponderosa is an easy tree to distinguish. Most of the trees around the Beaver Meadows entrance are ponderosa pine.

At the same elevation but in moister locations, such as north-facing shady slopes, dense stands of Douglas fir grow. These trees have thick, gray, corky bark and cones with scales sporting a "rat-tail" bract. Both ponderosa pine and Douglas fir are adapted to surviving relatively small fires at frequent, ten- to twenty-year intervals. Their thick bark helps protect them from light, "cool" fires. In fact, occasional fire is essential to maintaining healthy forests, and fire suppression, more than any other factor, has contributed to significant changes in tree density and numbers. Overstocked stands, in which fire has been excluded for an unnaturally long period of time, will burn hotter when fire is eventually introduced through either natural (lightning) or human means. Such fires can be bigger and more severe than those once experienced by these forests, prior to the era of significant human intervention.

Aspen and boulder, autumn in Moraine Park.

At slightly wetter and higher elevations, between 8,000 and 10,000 feet, forests of lodgepole pine grow. Lodgepole got its name from the use of its straight, narrow boles for teepee poles. It is also fire dependent, but unlike the ponderosa pine and Douglas fir, which are adapted to surviving fire, the lodgepole pine depends on larger, more severe burns to kill the overstory and provide a perfect seedbed for the growth of new trees. Fire intervals are several hundred years long, and while most green trees die, the heated lodgepole pine cones open up to shed their seeds a day or two after a fire has passed through. The next generation of pine upon the site is thereby established.

The aspen trees, with their fluttering leaves and white or light green trunks, mingle with lodgepole pine stands. In autumn, golden aspen leaves brighten entire hillsides. Aspen is another fire-adapted tree. Instead of relying upon seeds, it sprouts new shoots from its roots any time a fire, avalanche, or other disturbance kills the above-ground boles. Since a single root can send up numerous shoots, many aspen stands consist of clones, or genetically identical trees. Clones are relatively easy to identify in autumn when a small group of trees will all turn the same shade of yellow or orange at the same time.

In the wetter areas along streams and near timberline—from 11,000 to 11,800 feet, depending on slope exposure and protection from wind—are the pointed crowns that define the heavy-snow forests of subalpine fir and Englemann spruce. Both form twisted, wind-sheared stands at timberline. The fir has soft needles and a smooth, gray bark, while the red-barked spruce sports needles prickly to the touch. To remember the difference between these two trees, think of this catchy phrase: fir is friendly, spruce is spiny. Joining the spruce and fir on the highest wind-swept ridges are pockets of limber pine. These trees have needles in groups of five and roundish cones.

But it is the treeless, gale-buffeted alpine tundra that is Rocky Mountain's most unique plant community. Above timberline the last scraggly trees fall away, and what appears to be a grassy, flowered plain dominates. Here, the growing season may last four to six weeks at most, and short, mat-like, cushion plants, such as moss campion and phlox, brighten the landscape with colorful blooms. The tundra of Rocky Mountain National Park is particularly well developed compared to other parts of the West. Most of the park was not extensively grazed by domestic livestock. In addition, the considerable high-elevation terrain was left relatively level and untouched by glaciers during the last ice age, so that deep, rich soils have developed on these sites. Finally, the afternoon thunderstorms that characterize this region act as a natural irrigation system for tundra plants. Miles of alpine tundra are accessible from Trail Ridge Road, as well as from many trails within the park.

WILDLIFE

All of this scenery is enlivened by wildlife. Rocky Mountain National Park is home to considerable numbers of native species. Elk are the most abundant large mammal—and the most likely species for visitors to spot. In summer, the elk are widely scattered throughout the high country, but in early autumn, during the rutting season, they become easier to locate. The male elk, or bull, has massive antlers and calls to females in a high-pitched whistle, or "bugle."

Smaller, light brown in color, and numbering only about 800 individuals in the park are bighorn sheep. Although both males and females have horns, only the males wear the immense, curling head decorations that gives these animals their common name. Wild sheep favor more rugged terrain than elk. They frequently descend into Horseshoe Park to eat at mineral licks and can often be seen beside the road.

Sharing the park with both elk and bighorns in the summer are the grayish deer with the immense ears—appropriately named mule deer. Most deer, as well as most of the park's elk, migrate to lower, more snow-free elevations for the winter.

The other large member of the deer family found in the park is the long-legged moose. Moose, which are not native to Colorado, were introduced into the Kawuneeche Valley during the 1970s and are now relatively common in wetlands and willow patches along the North Fork of the Colorado River. Their long legs make it easier for them to forage in the deeper snows characteristic of the westside valleys.

At one time elk, bighorn sheep, and deer, along with now-

Porcupine in a winter snowstorm.

extinct bison, formed the prey base for large predators such as grizzly bear and wolf. Both animals were extirpated from Colorado; however, there is discussion about reintroducing wolves into the state, and Rocky Mountain National Park would likely be one of the choice locations. Today, the largest predators in the park are mountain lions, also known as cougars. Mountain lions hunt primarily deer and elk, capturing animals by stealth and surprise, not by chase. A highly secretive animal, it's unlikely that you will see a mountain lion in broad daylight. The same is true of the mountain lion's smaller cousin, the bobcat. Bobcat prey upon small birds and rodents, but hunt primarily at night.

More likely to be heard than seen is the coyote, whose yipping howl echoes throughout the park, particularly early in the morning and the evening. This grayish-red wild canid feeds mostly on small rodents, such as golden-mantled ground squirrels and meadow voles, but may occasionally take down prey as large as a deer or even an elk under the right circumstances.

A small population of black bear—estimated at 30 to 35 individuals—also roam the park, mostly in the forested areas. The predominantly rocky terrain does not constitute choice bear habitat, meaning that their numbers are limited. Despite the name, black bears come in a variety of colors, including brown, cinnamon, and blonde.

If you visit the high country, the yellow-bellied marmot, a relative of the groundhog, can often be seen sunning on rocks or scurrying among boulder piles. Sharing this rocky habitat is the pika, a small rabbitlike creature more often heard calling out a shrill "eek!" than actually seen.

A unique alpine resident is the chickenlike ptarmigan. Its plumage changes from brown in summer to white in winter, camouflaging it from predators.

THE FUTURE OF THE PARK

Like many national parks in the country, Rocky Mountain is suffering because its boundaries are not large enough to protect an entire ecosystem. Recent advances in our knowledge of ecological processes, such as wildfire, as well as a better understanding of the habitat necessary to prevent species

Elk (wapiti) bull, autumn.

extinction, point to the conclusion that only very large, interconnected wildland complexes can adequately provide long-term protection of important biological values. If Rocky Mountain National Park is to serve truly as an International Biosphere Reserve, the current borders of Rocky Mountain National Park will have to be expanded greatly, or, at least, management on surrounding lands will need to conform more completely with biological imperatives rather than economic dictates.

Acting upon recent scientific insights, some Colorado environmentalists have proposed expanding Rocky Mountain National Park as part of an ecosystem management complex, which would give priority to biological values and ecological processes throughout the Front Range and protect land from the plains to the high peaks. Migration corridors for elk and other wildlife would be protected or reestablished. Wolves would be

reintroduced. Livestock grazing may have to be eliminated from public lands surrounding the park to give greater use of these lands to native species such as bighorn sheep and elk. Wildfires would also be allowed to assume their former role as a major influence upon plant communities and nutrient cycling.

Nearly a hundred years ago, Enos Mills proposed making the entire Front Range into a park, but exploitive interests successfully vanquished his idea. As we approach the centennial anniversary of Rocky Mountain National Park, many people are beginning to believe that Mills's vision may be exactly what is necessary for the long-term survival of the park and its wild inhabitants. Without some adjustment in management, along the line of Mills's original park proposal, even the small portion of the Front Range that was set aside may well lose the very qualities that have drawn millions of visitors to this "rooftop of America."

Moss campion and granite.

Longs Peak seen from near Rock Cut on Trail Ridge Road.

SPRING
THE AWAKENING

Spring blossoms: lupine, yellow paintbrush, and golden alexander.   19

Stream in Hidden Valley.

The Ptarmigan Needles seen from Lake Nanita.

Meadow of golden banner in Moraine Park.   22

Sunrise from the shore of Sprague Lake.

Englemann spruce at tree-line, Trail Ridge.

Chasm Falls on Fall River.

Fall River Canyon, summer morning.

SUMMER

Longs Peak seen from Bear Lake.

Chasm Lake and Longs Peak, sunrise.

East Inlet at Paradise Creek.

Outlet of Crystal Lake, Mummy Range.   30

31   Aspen and blue columbine (Colorado's State Flower).

Mushroom Rocks along Tundra Nature Trail, Trail Ridge.

The Big Thompson River in Moraine Park, late summer.

Low clouds seen from Trail Ridge Road.   34

Alpine wildflowers on the tundra, Trail Ridge.

Hallett Peak seen from Dream Lake.

The Never Summer Range seen from Trail Ridge.

Aspens above Bear Lake in autumn color phase.

AUTUMN

Autumn along Glacier Creek.

Kawuneeche Valley, headwaters of the Colorado River.

Aspens along Glacier Creek Trail.

Aspens in Horseshoe Park.

Tundra and Longs Peak, Trail Ridge in autumn.

Mountain ash above Glacier Creek Trail.

Alberta Falls and aspens in autumn color.

Hallett Peak and Bear Lake, sunrise.

Aspens growing on Bierstadt Moraine.

The Mummy Range cloaked in autumn color.

Aspens and firs, late-autumn snowstorm.

Dawn light on Longs Peak from Moraine Park.

WINTER

Great horned owl huddled in bare branches.

Frozen beaver pond near Cub Lake Trail.

Loch Vale from the Loch, mid-winter.

Hallett Peak seen from near Glacier Creek, winter sunrise.   54

Mist and fog shrouded mountains as seen from near Bear Lake.

The view up Spruce Canyon from Moraine Park, mid-winter. 56

Aspen grove in winter cloak of snow.

The Mummy Range, winter sunrise.

Moonset and trees covered by newly fallen snow.

SPRING
THE RE-AWAKENING

Alpine buttercup emerging from snow, early spring.

"Krummholz" trees, late spring at tree-line. 61

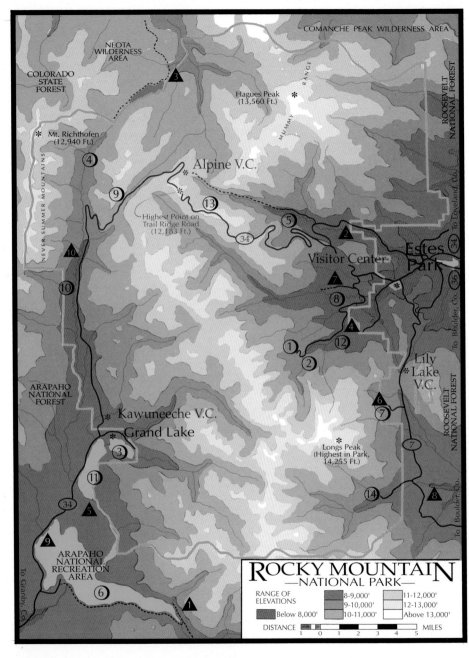

VISITOR CENTERS:

Alpine V.C.—June through September
Kawuneeche V.C.—Open all year
Lily Lake V.C.—Open May to October
Moraine Park Museum—May to Oct.
Park Headquarters and Visitor Center
   in Estes Park—Open all year

POINTS OF INTEREST

① Bear Lake
② Glacier Gorge/Alberta Falls Trailhead
③ Grand Lake
④ Headwaters of the Colorado River
⑤ Horseshoe Park
⑥ Lake Granby
⑦ Longs Peak Trailhead
⑧ Moraine Park
⑨ Milner Pass/Poudre Lake
⑩ Never Summer Ranch
⑪ Shadow Mountain Lake
⑫ Sprague Lake
⑬ Tundra Nature Trail
⑭ Wild Basin Trailhead

CAMPGROUNDS

▲1 Arapaho Bay (USFS)
▲2 Aspenglen
▲3 Corral Creek (USFS)
▲4 Glacier Basin
▲5 Green Ridge (USFS)
▲6 Longs Peak (Tents only)
▲7 Moraine Park
▲8 Olive Ridge (USFS)
▲9 Stillwater (USFS)
▲10 Timber Creek

ROCKY MOUNTAIN
—NATIONAL PARK—

RANGE OF ELEVATIONS

Below 8,000'	8-9,000'
9-10,000'	11-12,000'
10-11,000'	12-13,000'
	Above 13,000'

DISTANCE 1 0 1 2 3 4 5 MILES

FOR MORE INFORMATION

Superintendent
Rocky Mountain N.P.
Estes Park, CO 80517
(303) 586-2371

Rocky Mountain Nature Assoc.
Rocky Mountain N.P.
Estes Park, CO 80517
(303) 586-2371

Forest Supervisor
Roosevelt National Forest
161 Second St.
Estes Park, CO 80517
(303) 586-3440

Forest Supervisor
Arapaho National Forest
301 S. Howes
Fort Collins, CO 80521
(303) 482-5155

ACCOMMODATIONS

Chamber of Commerce
Estes Park, CO 80517
(303) 586-4431

Chamber of Commerce
Grand Lake, CO 80447
(303) 627-3372

Rocky Mountain Park Co.
PO Box 2680
Estes Park, CO 80517
(303) 586-9308

REGIONAL ATTRACTIONS

1. Badlands National Park/Black Hills, South Dakota
2. Canyon deChelly National Monument, Arizona
3. Canyonlands National Park/Glen Canyon
   National Recreation Area, Utah
4. Colorado National Monument, Colorado
5. Custer Battlefield National Monument, Montana
6. Devils Tower National Monument, Wyoming
7. Grand Teton National Park, Wyoming
8. Great Sand Dunes National Monument, Colorado
9. Mesa Verde National Park, Colorado
10. Petrified Forest National Park, Arizona
11. Yellowstone National Park, Wyoming

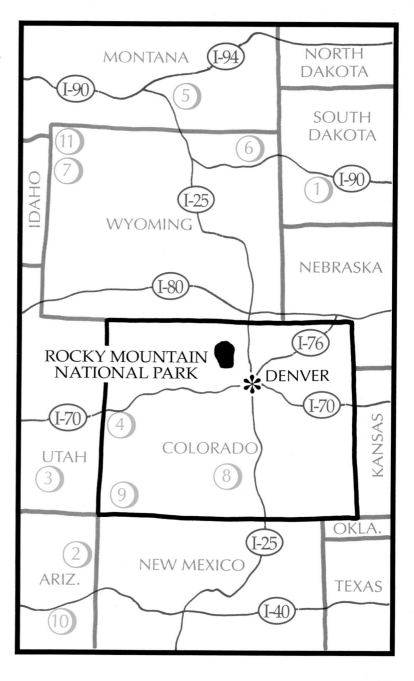

PHOTOGRAPHIC CREDITS

Frank S. Balthis: 16
Jim Battles (Dembinsky Photo Assoc.): 31
Willard Clay (Dembinsky Photo Assoc.): 33,49
Ed Cooper: 7,27,39,45
Kent & Donna Dannen: 28
Michael H. Francis: 10
Jeff Gnass: 26,40,48
Jenny Hager: 38
Dan & Cindy Hartman: 51
John H. Kieffer: 14,20,23,24,54,56,57
J.C. Leacock: 9,17,18,19,25,46
Mark & Jennifer Miller: Back Cover
Steve Mulligan: 50
Jeff Nicholas: Front Cover,13,42,43
Laurence Parent: 36,58,59
James Randklev: 2
Randall K. Roberts: 6,37
Tom Till: 61
Glenn Van Nimwegen: 35,47,60
Barbara Von Hoffman: 3(Left),11,55
John Ward: 3(Right),21,22,29,30,34,41,44,52,53
Jim Wilson: 8,32
George Wuerthner: 12

CREDITS

"The Rooftop of America" by George Wuerthner
Editor: Nicky Leach
Book Design by Jeff Nicholas
Photo Editor: Jeff Nicholas
Maps by Jeff Nicholas
Printing coordinated by TWP, Ltd., Berkeley, Ca.
Printed in Singapore, 1995

SUGGESTED READING

Benedict, Audrey D. *A Sierra Club Naturalist's Guide: The Southern Rockies.* San Francisco, CA: Sierra Club Books. 1991.

Buchholtz, C. W. *Rocky Mountain National Park: A History.* Boulder, CO: Colorado Associated University Press. 1983.

Chronic, Halka. *Roadside Geology of Colorado.* Missoula, MT: Mountain Press Publishing Company. 1980.

Hess, Karl. *Rocky Times in Rocky Mountain National Park.* Boulder, CO: University of Colorado. 1993.

Nelson, Ruth. *Plants of Rocky Mountain National Park.* Estes Park, CO: Rocky Mountain Nature Association. 1970.

Smithson, Michael. *Rocky Mountain: The Story Behind the Scenery.* Las Vegas, NV: KC Publications. 1986.

Veblen, Thomas and Diane Lorenz. *The Colorado Front Range: A Century of Ecological Change.* Salt Lake City, UT: University of Utah Press. 1991.

Warren, Scott. *Exploring Colorado's Wild Areas.* Seattle, WA: The Mountaineers. 1992.

Willard, Beatrice and Susan Foster. *A Roadside Guide to Rocky Mountain National Park.* Boulder, CO: Johnson Books. 1990.